TO WHOM MUCH IS GIVEN MUCH IS REQUIRED

LEADERSHIP, LEGACY, AND THE COST OF CALLING

PASTOR DR. CLAUDINE BENJAMIN

TO WHOM MUCH IS GIVEN. Copyright @ 2025. Pastor Dr. Claudine Benjamin. All rights reserved.

Published by:

Editor: Cleveland O. McLeish (Author C. Orville McLeish)

ISBN: 978-1-965635-78-0 (paperback)

This is not a book about theory—it is a call to action. It is a summons to live as one entrusted, to resist complacency, and to prepare for eternity with urgency and joy.

Whether you are a new believer longing for direction, a seasoned leader seeking renewal, or a Christian desiring to live faithfully in every area of life, this book will equip you to finish your stewardship well and hear the words of your Master: **"Well done, good and faithful servant... enter thou into the joy of thy Lord."**

About the Author

Pastor Claudine Benjamin is a servant of God, a passionate preacher, teacher, and author whose life and ministry are devoted to the urgent call of the great commission. With a prophetic voice for this generation, she carries a burden to see souls saved, disciples made, and the body of Christ reignited with fire for evangelism.

Known for her ability to teach biblical truths with clarity and conviction, Pastor Claudine writes with both urgency and compassion, drawing from scripture, personal experience, and the leading of the Holy Spirit. Her books are marked by a prophetic edge, practical application, and a deep desire to equip believers to rise to the responsibility entrusted to them—"for to whom much is given, much is required" **(see Luke 12:48)**.

She has dedicated her ministry to strengthening churches, empowering leaders, and helping believers discover their purpose and walk in obedience to Christ. Beyond the pulpit and the written page, Pastor Claudine is also a mentor, intercessor, and encourager, pouring into the lives of those who are navigating storms, pursuing their calling, or seeking restoration in Christ.

Pastor Benjamin's ministry carries a burden for revival in the church and transformation in the world. Her writing weaves together biblical truth, practical application, and a prophetic call to action. Whether addressing church hurt, storms of life, or the call to evangelism, her heartbeat is clear: Christ must be glorified, souls must be won, and believers must live ready for His return.

When not preaching or writing, Pastor Benjamin finds joy in prayer, fellowship, and encouraging the body of Christ to rise into its full calling.

Her mission is clear: to compel men and women everywhere to embrace the saving grace of Jesus Christ and to live fully for Him until He returns.

Acknowledgment

I give all honor and glory to the Lord, the One who entrusted me with this assignment and equipped me to carry it through. Truly, **"to whom much is given, much is required,"** and I recognize the sacred responsibility that comes with the gifts, opportunities, and calling He has placed upon my life. Without His strength, this work would not be possible.

To my family, whose love, prayers, and encouragement carried me through every moment—thank you for standing beside me with patience and faith.

To my spiritual mentors and fellow laborers in the kingdom, your counsel and example have continually reminded me of the weight of the call and the joy of service. I am also deeply grateful to every prayer warrior and supporter who believed in the vision and covered this journey with intercession.

Finally, I acknowledge you, the reader. May these words challenge and inspire you to rise to the level of responsibility God has placed upon your life, walking faithfully in obedience to His will.

Dedication

This work is dedicated first and foremost to the Lord Jesus Christ, my Savior and Master, who has given me both the gift of life and the privilege of service.

I also dedicate it to every believer who recognizes the truth of Luke 12:48 and desires to live a life of stewardship, obedience, and accountability before God. May you be reminded that the measure of your blessing is also the measure of your responsibility.

And to future generations—may you pick up the mantle, run with the vision, and never forget that much has been entrusted to you, and much will be required.

Table of Contents

Part IV

Stewardship in the World

Part V

The Eternal Perspective of Stewardship

Part VI

Living with Purposeful Stewardship

Introduction

The Weight of Responsibility in Blessing

Every blessing carries a burden. Every gift carries a weight. Every calling carries a cross. When Jesus declared in Luke 12:48, **"For everyone to whom much is given, from him much will be required; and to whom much has been committed, of him they will ask the more." (NKJV)**, He was not merely speaking a proverb—He was laying down a kingdom principle. Blessings are not random; they are deliberate. And because they are deliberate, they demand accountability.

We often pray for more—more anointing, more opportunities, more influence, more provision. But God's increase always arrives wrapped in responsibility. To receive much is to shoulder much. To carry much is to answer for much. Heaven never entrusts resources lightly because God's kingdom operates on stewardship, not ownership.

BLESSING AND ACCOUNTABILITY GO HAND IN HAND

James 1:17 reminds us, **"Every good gift and every perfect gift is from above, and comes down from the Father of lights, with** whom there is no variation or shadow of turning." (NKJV). This means that everything we possess—our time, health, finances, talents, wisdom, influence, even our very breath—is entrusted to us by God. Nothing is truly ours. We are managers, not masters. And God, the Giver, will one day call us to account.

The Apostle Paul wrote in 1 Corinthians 4:2, "Moreover it is required in stewards that one be found faithful." (NKJV). That word *required* echoes Jesus' own teaching. Faithfulness is not optional; it is expected. God measures not by how much we hold in our hands but by how we use what we've been given.

THE DANGER OF MISMANAGING BLESSING

Blessings, when mismanaged, become curses. Talent without submission leads to pride. Wealth without generosity breeds greed. Influence without integrity destroys souls. The higher God lifts us, the greater the fall if we neglect responsibility. That is why the parable of the talents (see Matthew 25:14–30) ends with such a sobering warning: the servant who buried his talent was not excused—he was condemned. Neglect is as dangerous as rebellion.

Many want God's favor without God's accountability. But kingdom stewardship doesn't work that way. To receive the crown, we must also carry the cross. To enjoy the glory, we must embrace the responsibility.

A CALL TO THE READER

This book is not merely about understanding a principle—it is about embracing a lifestyle. It is a call to the believer who has been saved by grace, filled with the Spirit, and blessed beyond measure, to live in alignment with heaven's expectation. It will explore:

- The biblical foundation of accountability.
- The stewardship of spiritual gifts, talents, and opportunities.
- The responsibility of leaders and influencers.
- The management of resources, time, and relationships.
- The consequences of neglect and the rewards of faithfulness.

It is a reminder that salvation is free, but discipleship is costly. Blessing is abundant, but stewardship is required.

LIVING WITH ETERNITY IN VIEW

One day, we will all stand before the judgment seat of Christ (**see 2 Corinthians 5:10**). On that day, excuses will vanish, and only faithfulness will matter. Titles won't matter, but testimony will. Wealth won't matter, but works will. Popularity won't matter, but purity will.

When the Master returns, will He find us faithful? Will He say, **"Well done, good and faithful servant" (see Matthew 25:21)**, or will He declare us unfaithful stewards? The answer depends on how we live with what we have been given today.

This book is an invitation and a warning, a comfort and a challenge. To whom much is given, much is required. The question is—are we living up to the weight of what has been entrusted to us?

REFLECTION

1. What blessings in your life do you sometimes take for granted?

2. How have you viewed responsibility—as a burden, or as a privilege?

3. If God were to ask you today for an account of your time, talent, and treasure, what would your answer be?

4. In what ways do you sense God calling you higher in stewardship and faithfulness?

PRAYER

Heavenly Father, I acknowledge that everything I have comes from You. My breath, my strength, my gifts, and my opportunities are not my own—they are entrusted to me by Your hand. Lord, forgive me for the times I have mismanaged or neglected what You gave me. Today, I make a fresh commitment to live as a faithful steward. Please help me carry the weight of responsibility with joy and humility. Teach me to serve with integrity, to love with compassion, and to labor with diligence. May my life reflect that I understand the seriousness of Your Word: **"To whom much is given, much is required."** Prepare my heart for the journey through this book and shape me into a servant who lives ready for Your return. In Jesus' name. Amen.

Part I

The Principle of Accountability

Chapter 1

The Biblical Foundation of "Much Is Required"

A KINGDOM PRINCIPLE, NOT A SUGGESTION

When Jesus declared, **"For everyone to whom much is given, from him much will be required" (Luke 12:48 - NKJV),** He wasn't offering a proverb for wise living; He was announcing a kingdom law. This principle flows through the entire narrative of scripture: blessing and responsibility are inseparable.

God never gives gifts for personal hoarding. He gives with the expectation that His children will multiply what has been entrusted. Just as the sun does not shine for itself, so the believer's gifts, opportunities, and blessings are never meant to terminate with them—they are meant to serve the purposes of God.

THE PARABLE OF THE TALENTS: A PICTURE OF ACCOUNTABILITY

One of the clearest biblical illustrations of this principle is found in the Parable of the Talents (**see Matthew 25:14–30**). In the story, a master entrusted three servants with varying amounts of money: five talents, two talents, and one talent.

- The first two servants invested wisely, doubling what they had been given.

- The third buried his talent out of fear, refusing to risk or labor with what had been entrusted.

When the master returned, he commended the faithful servants: **"Well done, good and faithful servant. You have been faithful over a few things, I will make you ruler over many things."** But to the negligent servant, he declared condemnation, casting him into outer darkness.

This parable highlights three truths about responsibility:

1. **God gives different measures**—not everyone receives the same, but everyone receives something.

2. **God expects increase**—He is not satisfied with maintenance; He expects fruitfulness.

3. **God will call for an account**—faithfulness brings reward, but negligence brings judgment.

OLD TESTAMENT WITNESS: ISRAEL'S RESPONSIBILITY

God's dealings with Israel further reveal this principle. In Amos 3:2, the Lord declared to His chosen people: **"You only have I known of all the families of the earth; Therefore I will punish you for all your iniquities." (NKJV).** Israel's privilege of being God's elect nation was accompanied by greater accountability.

To Israel was given the Law, the covenant, the promises, and the prophetic voice. But with these blessings came strict requirements: to walk in holiness and obedience. When they failed, judgment was swifter and stricter, not because God was unfair, but because **"to whom much is given, much is required."**

NEW TESTAMENT WITNESS: THE CHURCH'S ACCOUNTABILITY

The church carries an even weightier responsibility than Israel. We have received the fullness of revelation in Christ, the indwelling of the Holy Spirit, and the authority of the Word.

- The early disciples were entrusted with the gospel, and they carried it with urgency, even unto death.

- Paul reminded the Corinthians: **"Moreover it is required in stewards that one be found faithful." (1 Corinthians 4:2 - NKJV).**

- James warns, **"My brethren, let not many of you become teachers, knowing that we shall receive a stricter judgment." (James 3:1 - NKJV).**

The more revelation we walk in, the greater the responsibility we bear.

PRACTICAL APPLICATION: MODERN EXAMPLES

This principle still speaks today:

- The educated believer is responsible to use their knowledge for kingdom advancement.

- The wealthy believer is accountable to use their resources to bless others, not just themselves.

- The leader or pastor is responsible not just for their soul, but for those entrusted to their care.

- The Spirit-filled believer is accountable to walk in holiness and to witness boldly.

Neglect in any of these areas is not a light matter. It is a failure in stewardship.

LIVING WITH THE PRINCIPLE IN VIEW

Understanding this principle shifts our perspective. Instead of asking, *"What do I have?"* we begin asking, *"What am I doing with what I have?"* Instead of longing for more, we first seek to be faithful with the little entrusted to us.

Faithfulness today prepares us for responsibility tomorrow. The servant who was faithful over five talents was made ruler over ten cities (**see Luke 19:17**). God multiplies responsibility for those who steward well.

REFLECTION

1. What has God entrusted to you—time, talents, resources, influence—that you are currently stewarding well?

2. Where are you burying your "talent" out of fear, procrastination, or neglect?

3. How would your life change if you lived daily as though you will give an account to God?

PRAYER

Lord, open my eyes to see all that You have placed in my hands. Forgive me for the times I have hidden, neglected, or misused Your gifts. Teach me to live with a sober awareness that I will one day stand before You and give an account. Please help me to be faithful in small things, so that I may be trusted with greater things. Strengthen me to serve You with diligence, wisdom, and humility. May I be found faithful when the Master returns. In Jesus' name. Amen.

Chapter 2

God's Justice and Human Responsibility

A JUST GOD WHO REQUIRES JUSTLY

God is not a tyrant who demands the impossible. His requirements are always in proportion to the light, opportunity, and resources given. Romans 2:12–16 shows this clearly: **"For as many as have sinned without law will also perish without law, and as many as have sinned in the law will be judged by the law (for not the hearers of the law are just in the sight of God, but the doers of the law will be justified; or when Gentiles, who do not have the law, by nature do the things in the law, these, although not having the law, are a law to themselves, who show the work of the law written in their hearts, their conscience also bearing witness, and between themselves their thoughts accusing or else excusing them) in the day when God will judge the secrets of men by Jesus Christ, according to my gospel." (NKJV).**

This passage reveals a principle of divine justice:

- Those with little knowledge are judged by the little they know.

- Those with much knowledge are judged by the much they know.

God's justice is precise. He never measures us against someone else's light, but against our own. Yet the sobering truth remains: *the more we have been given, the greater our accountability before Him.*

THE JUSTICE OF GREATER JUDGMENT

Amos 3:2 records God's words to Israel: **"You only have I known of all the families of the earth; Therefore I will punish you for all your iniquities." (NKJV).**

Israel was chosen, privileged, and set apart. They received God's Law, God's covenant, and God's presence. But these privileges did not exempt them from judgment; instead, they increased their responsibility. God was saying: *"Because I gave you more, I require more from you."*

This is the consistent pattern of scripture:

- Angels who rebelled were judged swiftly (**see 2 Peter 2:4**).

- Priests who defiled the sanctuary faced stricter punishment (**see Leviticus 10:1–2**).

- Leaders and teachers are warned they will be judged more strictly (**see James 3:1**).

Privilege always increases accountability.

JUSTICE IN THE TEACHINGS OF JESUS

Jesus Himself reinforced this principle. In Luke 10:13–14 He declared:

> **"Woe to you, Chorazin! Woe to you, Bethsaida! For if the mighty works which were done in you had been done in Tyre and Sidon, they would have repented long ago, sitting in sackcloth and ashes. But it will be more tolerable for Tyre and Sidon at the judgment than for you." (NKJV).**

Why such a strong statement? Because Chorazin and Bethsaida had greater exposure to the ministry of Christ. They saw miracles, heard His words, and witnessed His power, yet they rejected Him. Therefore, their judgment would be greater.

This reminds us that access to truth is not neutral. Every sermon we hear, every scripture we read, and every opportunity we are given increases our accountability before God.

MODERN APPLICATION: LEVELS OF RESPONSIBILITY

- The unbeliever who never heard the gospel will be judged according to conscience and creation (**see Romans 1:20**).

- The churchgoer who has heard sermons for years will be judged by their response to the Word they consistently received.

- The leader who has been entrusted with guiding souls will face stricter judgment for every decision, teaching, and example they set.

- The nation saturated with Bibles and churches carries heavier accountability than those who live with little access to God's Word.

This principle should not make us fearful but should awaken us to the seriousness of what we have received. God's justice ensures He never requires unfairly, but His justice also ensures He never overlooks responsibility.

THE BALANCE OF JUSTICE AND MERCY

God's justice never operates apart from His mercy. While He requires much, He also provides grace to meet His requirements. Philippians 2:13 reminds us: **"for it is God who works in you both to will and to do for His good pleasure." (NKJV).**

- Justice says: "You must."
- Mercy says: "I will help you."
- Grace says: "You can."

The believer must therefore never excuse irresponsibility by hiding behind weakness, because the Spirit of God supplies strength for obedience.

LIVING WITH SOBRIETY AND HOPE

Understanding God's justice should produce two things in us:

1. **Sobriety** – A seriousness about how we live, knowing every decision counts before God.

2. **Hope** – A confidence that God's requirements are not impossible, because He equips us with grace to fulfill them.

We are not judged by comparison, but by stewardship. Our question should never be, *"Do I have as much as them?"* but rather, *"Am I faithful with what I have been given?"*

REFLECTION

1. How does knowing God's justice is fair change the way you view His requirements?

2. In what ways has God entrusted you with greater revelation (knowledge of the Word, spiritual experiences, opportunities)?

3. Are you living as though you will one day give an account for that greater light?

PRAYER

Righteous Father, I thank You that You are just in all Your ways. You never require more than You provide. You never demand beyond what You have given. Forgive me for the times I have taken lightly the blessings, teachings, and opportunities placed in my hands. Lord, help me to live with a sober awareness of my responsibility. Keep me from comparing myself to others, and teach me to be faithful with what You have entrusted to me. Strengthen me by Your Spirit to walk in obedience, knowing that Your justice is always balanced by Your mercy. In Jesus' name. Amen.

Chapter 3

Gifts, Talents, and the Call to Stewardship

EVERY GIFT COMES WITH A PURPOSE

Every human being is born with a measure of ability, opportunity, and potential. But when someone comes into Christ, they also receive spiritual gifts—supernatural endowments from the Holy Spirit to serve, edify, and advance the kingdom.

The Bible is clear: **"As each one has received a gift, minister it to one another, as good stewards of the manifold grace of God." (1 Peter 4:10 - NKJV).** Notice the word *stewards*. A steward doesn't own the gift; they manage it. That means our gifts are not ours to boast in, but God's to work through.

THE PARABLE OF THE TALENTS REVISITED

The Parable of the Talents (**see Matthew 25:14–30**) is more than a story about money. It is a picture of stewardship in every form:

- The five-talent servant represents those with abundant resources and opportunities.

- The two-talent servant shows us that God values faithfulness over volume—he was rewarded equally to the five-talent servant because he multiplied what he had.

- The one-talent servant warns us of the danger of neglect, fear, and laziness.

The lesson is sobering: *God does not measure us against each other, but against our faithfulness to what we were given.*

IDENTIFYING OUR GIFTS

Some believers say, *"I don't have much to offer."* But scripture disagrees. Every believer has something entrusted to them. Gifts may differ in type and visibility, but none are insignificant.

- **Spiritual Gifts (see 1 Corinthians 12:7–11):** wisdom, knowledge, faith, healing, miracles, prophecy, tongues, discernment.

- **Natural Talents:** teaching, leadership, craftsmanship, music, organization, creativity.

- **Opportunities and Influence:** relationships, networks, platforms, open doors.

Romans 12:6 reminds us: **"Having then gifts differing according to the grace that is given to us, let us use them: if prophecy, let us prophesy in proportion to our faith;" (NKJV).** The problem is not a lack of gifting, it is often a lack of willingness to use what has been entrusted.

THE DANGER OF NEGLECTING GIFTS

Neglect leads to spiritual decay. Paul warned Timothy: **"Neglect not the gift that is in thee" (see 1 Timothy 4:14).** Gifts left dormant atrophy. Talents buried are wasted. Opportunities ignored never return the same way.

Neglect can stem from:

- Fear – "What if I fail?"
- Comparison – "I'm not as good as them."
- Pride – "I don't need to use this for anyone else."
- Laziness – "I'll do it later."

But each of these is dangerous, because they insult the Giver by devaluing the gift.

STEWARDSHIP REQUIRES MULTIPLICATION

Faithful stewardship is not passive—it requires increase. God expects us to cultivate, sharpen, and multiply our gifts. Like muscles, gifts grow with use. Like seeds, talents multiply when planted.

- The singer must sing to edify.
- The teacher must study to impart truth.
- The intercessor must pray faithfully for breakthrough.
- The leader must shepherd with diligence.

Every act of stewardship positions us for greater responsibility. **"you have been faithful over a few things, I will make you ruler over many things." (Matthew 25:23 - NKJV).**

33

MODERN EXAMPLES OF STEWARDSHIP

- A believer with the gift of hospitality opening their home to disciple young Christians.

- A skilled professional using their expertise to serve their church or community.

- A young person using social media not just for entertainment, but to spread the gospel.

- A wealthy business owner funding missionary efforts in unreached areas.

These examples show that stewardship is not limited to the pulpit—it touches every area of life.

THE CALL TO ACCOUNTABILITY

At the Judgment Seat of Christ (**see 2 Corinthians 5:10**), we will not be asked, *"What did you have?"* but rather, *"What did you do with what you had?"* The size of the gift is not the issue; the faithfulness in using it is.

Therefore, every believer must ask:

- Am I maximizing my spiritual gifts?

- Am I using my natural talents for God's glory?

- Am I stewarding the opportunities and influence entrusted to me?

34

REFLECTION

1. What gifts, talents, or opportunities has God entrusted to you?

2. In what ways have you multiplied them? In what ways have you neglected them?

3. What steps can you take this week to actively steward one area of gifting more faithfully?

PRAYER

Father, thank You for the gifts You have placed in my life. Forgive me for the times I have neglected or compared them. Teach me to see every talent, opportunity, and influence as a trust from Your hand. Please help me to use them for service, not self. May my gifts never lie dormant, but be multiplied for Your glory. Empower me by Your Spirit to be faithful in stewardship, so that on the day of reckoning I may hear You say, "Well done." In Jesus' name. Amen.

Chapter 4

The Balance of Grace and Duty

GRACE DOES NOT CANCEL RESPONSIBILITY

One of the greatest misunderstandings in the church today is the misuse of grace. Some believers treat grace as an excuse for laziness, compromise, or irresponsibility. They say, *"I don't have to do anything, God has done it all."* While it is true that salvation is by grace alone through faith (**see Ephesians 2:8–9**), that same passage continues: **"For we are His workmanship, created in Christ Jesus for good works, which God prepared beforehand that we should walk in them." (Ephesians 2:10 - NKJV).**

Grace saves us, but grace also summons us to action. It redeems us from sin, but it also recruits us for service.

PAUL'S UNDERSTANDING OF GRACE AND DUTY

Paul is perhaps the strongest preacher of grace in the New Testament, yet he also carried the heaviest sense of duty.

In 1 Corinthians 15:10 he declared: **"But by the grace of God I am what I am, and His grace toward me was not in vain; but I labored more abundantly than they all, yet not I, but the grace of God which was with me." (NKJV).**

- Grace made him who he was.
- Grace demanded that he not waste it.
- Grace energized his labor.

This is the balance: *grace empowers our duty, and duty honors grace.*

GRACE IS A TEACHER, NOT JUST A GIFT

Titus 2:11–12 says: **"For the grace of God that brings salvation has appeared to all men, teaching us that, denying ungodliness and worldly lusts, we should live soberly, righteously, and godly in the present age." (NKJV).**

Notice that grace teaches. It does not merely excuse sin; it trains us to live differently. Grace without responsibility is counterfeit grace. True grace transforms the heart and equips the believer to fulfill God's requirements joyfully.

THE DANGER OF DUTY WITHOUT GRACE

On the other hand, some fall into the opposite error—trying to live by duty without depending on grace. This leads to:

- Legalism – serving out of fear, rules, and self-effort.
- Burnout – laboring without joy or empowerment.

- Pride – boasting in works rather than glorifying God.

Duty without grace is slavery. Grace without duty is irresponsibility. The kingdom requires the marriage of both.

JESUS: THE PERFECT EXAMPLE OF GRACE AND DUTY

Jesus embodied this balance. He was full of grace and truth (**see John 1:14**). His life reflected:

- Grace: freely healing the sick, forgiving sinners, and showing compassion.

- Duty: faithfully praying, fasting, obeying the Father, even to the cross.

He did not choose between grace and duty; He lived both perfectly. His example shows us that the Spirit-filled life is not passive but active, not legalistic but empowered.

PRACTICAL WAYS TO WALK IN BALANCE

1. **Depend Daily on Grace** – Begin every task by acknowledging your need for God's strength.

2. **Embrace Discipline as Worship** – See prayer, fasting, service, and holiness not as burdens but as joyful responses to grace.

3. **Reject Both Extremes** – Avoid the trap of careless grace ("I don't have to do anything") and the trap of crushing legalism ("It all depends on me").

4. **Labor with Love** – Remember that duty motivated by love for God is not drudgery but delight.

MODERN EXAMPLE

Think of a believer who sings beautifully.

- Grace gave the voice.

- Duty requires practice, discipline, and service to the church.

- If they rely only on grace without practice, the gift is wasted.

- If they rely only on practice without grace, the ministry is powerless.

- But when grace and duty unite, the gift becomes fruitful and life-changing.

LIVING IN PARTNERSHIP WITH GOD

Philippians 2:12–13 captures the balance perfectly: **"Therefore, my beloved, as you have always obeyed, not as in my presence only, but now much more in my absence, work out your own salvation with fear and trembling; for it is God who works in you both to will and to do for His good pleasure." (NKJV).**

- Verse 12 emphasizes duty: work out.
- Verse 13 emphasizes grace: God works in you.

We work because God is working in us. Our labor is not self-generated but Spirit-empowered.

REFLECTION

1. Have you leaned more toward grace without responsibility, or duty without grace?

2. How does understanding the balance free you from both fear and laziness?

3. What is one area in your life where you need to depend more on grace, and one area where you need to exercise more discipline?

PRAYER

Lord, thank You for Your amazing grace that saved me. Thank You that I did not earn it, and I cannot repay it. Yet I know this grace is not a license to neglect my responsibility—it is the power to fulfill it. Forgive me for the times I have leaned into extremes, either living carelessly or striving in my own strength. Teach me to walk in the balance of grace and duty. Empower me to serve joyfully, obey willingly, and labor faithfully. May everything I do be fueled by Your Spirit and offered back to You in love. In Jesus' name. Amen.

Part II

Stewardship of the Inner Life

Stewardship of Our Own Life

Chapter 5

Spiritual Gifts: Not for Show but for Service

THE PURPOSE OF GIFTS

The church today often celebrates the spectacular side of spiritual gifts—prophecy, healing, tongues, miracles—while forgetting their central purpose: service. Paul writes in 1 Corinthians 12:7, **"But the manifestation of the Spirit is given to each one for the profit of all:" (NKJV).**

That phrase to *profit withal* means gifts are meant to benefit others, not ourselves. Spiritual gifts are tools, not trophies. They are for ministry, not manipulation. They are for edifying the body of Christ, not elevating an individual's name.

THE DANGER OF USING GIFTS FOR SHOW

The Corinthian church struggled with this very issue. They abounded in spiritual gifts, yet Paul rebuked them for pride, disorder, and immaturity. Their gatherings became a contest of who could speak in tongues the most, who could prophesy the loudest, or who seemed the most "anointed."

This misuse reveals two dangers:

1. Pride – Viewing gifts as proof of spiritual superiority.

2. Performance – Using gifts as a stage act instead of a channel of God's power.

Jesus warned of such misuse in Matthew 7:22–23: **"Many will say to Me in that day, 'Lord, Lord, have we not prophesied in Your name, cast out demons in Your name, and done many wonders in Your name?' And then I will declare to them, 'I never knew you; depart from Me, you who practice lawlessness!'" (NKJV).**

The gifts are real, but without love and holiness, they profit nothing.

LOVE: THE MORE EXCELLENT WAY

1 Corinthians 13, the "love chapter," is not a romantic poem—it is Paul's correction to the Corinthians about gifts. He made it clear:

- Without love, tongues are noise.
- Without love, prophecy is empty.
- Without love, generosity and sacrifice mean nothing.

Love is the atmosphere in which gifts operate effectively. Gifts without love destroy. Gifts with love edify.

EXAMPLES OF GIFTS IN SERVICE

- A believer with the gift of healing prays for the sick, not for applause, but out of compassion.

- A prophet speaks the truth in love, pointing people to Christ, not to themselves.

- A teacher explains scripture simply so others can understand, not to sound intellectual.

- An intercessor prays faithfully behind the scenes, unseen by men but honored by God.

These examples remind us that gifts are not entertainment—they are assignments.

THE STEWARDSHIP OF GIFTS

Being entrusted with a spiritual gift means we must:

1. **Cultivate it** – Gifts grow with use and maturity (**see 2 Timothy 1:6**).

2. **Submit it** – Gifts must always operate under the authority of Christ and scripture.

3. **Sanctify it** – The vessel matters as much as the gift; purity protects power.

4. **Multiply it** – Faithful use of a gift leads to an increase in effectiveness and responsibility.

The Spirit never gives gifts for self-glorification but for kingdom edification.

MODERN WARNING: CELEBRITY CHRISTIANITY

Today's church culture often elevates giftedness above character. Some measure success by how "anointed" a service feels rather than how transformed lives become. This is dangerous. Charisma without character ruins ministries. Power without purity destroys lives.

A true steward understands that the gift is nothing without the Giver. As John the Baptist declared: **"He must increase, but I must decrease." (John 3:30 - NKJV).**

LIVING AS A SERVANT WITH GIFTS

Spiritual gifts reach their full potential when used in humility and service. Jesus modeled this perfectly: though filled with the Spirit without measure, He washed His disciples' feet (**see John 13:14–15**).

The call is clear: *the greater the gift, the deeper the service.*

REFLECTION

1. Have you ever been tempted to use your gifts for recognition instead of service?

2. Do you see your gifts as a trust from God or as a tool for self-promotion?

3. How can you better use your gifts this week to serve others with love?

PRAYER

Lord, thank You for the spiritual gifts You have entrusted to me. Forgive me if I have ever used them to seek attention, approval, or personal glory. Please help me to remember that every gift is a tool for service, not a trophy for pride. Teach me to walk in love, humility, and obedience so that my gifts may build up Your church and bring glory to Your name. May I never be found performing, but always serving. In Jesus' name. Amen.

Chapter 6

The Cost of Discipleship

FOLLOWING JESUS COMES AT A PRICE

When Jesus called His disciples, He didn't promise them comfort, applause, or earthly reward. Instead, He told them: **"If anyone desires to come after Me, let him deny himself, and take up his cross daily, and follow Me." (Luke 9:23 - NKJV).**

Discipleship is not a casual decision; it is a costly surrender. It requires more than church attendance or verbal confession—it demands our lives. Salvation is free, but discipleship will cost us everything.

JESUS' HARD SAYINGS ON DISCIPLESHIP

In Luke 14:26–27, Jesus declared: **"If anyone comes to Me and does not hate his father and mother, wife and children, brothers and sisters, yes, and his own life also, he cannot be My disciple. And whoever does not bear his cross and come after Me cannot be My disciple." (NKJV).**

These words are not about literal hatred but about priority. Jesus was teaching that loyalty to Him must outweigh every earthly attachment—even family, reputation, and life itself.

He continued in verse 28: **"For which of you, intending to build a tower, does not sit down first and count the cost, whether he has enough to finish it—" (NKJV).**

In other words, discipleship is an investment—it must be considered, counted, and embraced with sobriety.

WHAT THE COST INVOLVES

1. **Self-Denial** – Saying no to our own desires, ambitions, and fleshly appetites (**see Galatians 2:20**).

2. **Sacrifice** – Giving up comfort, possessions, or status when obedience requires it (**see Matthew 19:21**).

3. **Suffering** – Enduring persecution, trials, or rejection for Christ's sake (**see 2 Timothy 3:12**).

4. **Separation** – Walking away from relationships, environments, or opportunities that conflict with God's call (**see 2 Corinthians 6:17**).

BIBLICAL EXAMPLES OF COSTLY DISCIPLESHIP

- Abraham left his homeland and family to follow God's call (**see Genesis 12:1–4**).

- Moses forsook Egypt's riches, choosing to suffer with God's people (**see Hebrews 11:24–25**).

- The disciples left their nets, boats, and businesses immediately when Jesus called them (**see Matthew 4:19–20**).

- Paul counted all things loss compared to knowing Christ (**see Philippians 3:7–8**).

Every true disciple has a testimony of cost.

THE REWARD OF PAYING THE COST

Jesus also promised that no sacrifice made for Him goes unrewarded. In Mark 10:29–30, He said: **"there is no one who has left house or brothers or sisters or father or mother or wife or children or lands, for My sake and the gospel's, who shall not receive a hundredfold now in this time—houses and brothers and sisters and mothers and children and lands, with persecutions—and in the age to come, eternal life." (NKJV).**

The cost is real, but the reward is greater. We lose nothing of eternal value when we surrender to Christ.

MODERN APPLICATIONS OF THE COST

- A believer refusing unethical practices at work, even if it costs a promotion.

- A young person choosing holiness over popularity in school or on social media.

- A missionary leaving behind comfort to reach unreached people.

- A Christian family enduring ridicule for holding fast to biblical truth.

Every generation must rediscover the cost of discipleship. The modern church often emphasizes blessing without cost, but Christ never separated the two.

CARRYING THE CROSS DAILY

The cost is not paid once; it is carried daily. Luke 9:23 emphasizes **"take up his cross daily."** Every day we face choices—deny self or indulge self, obey God or follow flesh. Discipleship is not a single sacrifice, but a lifestyle of surrender.

REFLECTION

1. What has following Jesus cost you so far?

2. Are there areas where you resist surrender because the price feels too high?

3. How can you embrace daily cross-bearing with joy instead of reluctance?

PRAYER

Lord Jesus, I thank You that You paid the ultimate cost for my salvation. You denied Yourself, took up the cross, and endured suffering for me. Now You call me to follow in Your steps. Forgive me for the times I have wanted the crown without the cross, the blessing without the cost. Teach me to deny myself daily, to embrace sacrifice willingly, and to endure suffering faithfully. Strengthen me to count the cost and still choose You every time. May my life declare that You are worth more than anything I leave behind. In Your name. Amen.

Chapter 7

Prayer, Fasting, and the Secret Place

THE POWER OF THE SECRET PLACE

Jesus taught: **"But you, when you pray, go into your room, and when you have shut your door, pray to your Father who is in the secret place; and your Father who sees in secret will reward you openly." (Matthew 6:6 - NKJV).**

The secret place is where strength is gained, direction is given, and burdens are lifted. Public ministry is fueled by private devotion. Without intimacy with God, spiritual gifts become empty, discipleship becomes heavy, and service becomes hollow. The secret place is where responsibility is renewed.

PRAYER: THE BREATH OF THE DISCIPLE

Prayer is not optional for those to whom much has been given. It is the very oxygen of stewardship. Luke 18:1 says: **"men always ought to pray and not lose heart." (NKJV).**

- **Prayer aligns us** – It keeps our hearts in tune with God's will.

- **Prayer equips us** – It arms us against temptation and spiritual warfare.

- **Prayer humbles us** – It reminds us that without God, we can do nothing.

Jesus Himself, though sinless and full of the Spirit, continually withdrew to pray (**see Mark 1:35, Luke 5:16**). If the Son of God needed the discipline of prayer, how much more do we?

FASTING: THE DISCIPLINE OF DENIAL

Fasting is the deliberate denial of physical appetite to seek spiritual strength. Jesus did not say "if you fast" but "when you fast" (**see Matthew 6:16**). It is an expectation, not an option.

Fasting sharpens spiritual sensitivity, breaks chains of bondage, and humbles the soul before God. Isaiah 58:6 calls fasting a tool to **"loose the bonds of wickedness, to undo the heavy burdens, to let the oppressed go free." (NKJV).**

Through fasting, we lay down comfort to take up power. It is the hidden sacrifice that produces open strength.

THE PARTNERSHIP OF PRAYER AND FASTING

Prayer and fasting are often most powerful together. Jesus told His disciples when they struggled to cast out a demon: **"This kind can come out by nothing but prayer and fasting." (Mark 9:29).**

Some responsibilities God gives us will never be carried out without a deeper life of consecration. To whom much is given in authority, influence, or calling, much is required in prayer and fasting.

THE REWARD OF THE SECRET PLACE

Jesus promised that what is done in secret will be rewarded openly. This means:

- Hidden prayers produce visible breakthroughs.
- Private fasts produce public power.
- Secret devotion produces lasting fruit.

Moses' forty days on the mountain were unseen, but the glory on his face was undeniable (**see Exodus 34:29**). Elijah's prayers in private shut and opened the heavens (**see 1 Kings 17:1, James 5:17–18**).

The measure of our secret life determines the measure of our public effectiveness.

MODERN APPLICATION: DISTRACTIONS VS. DEVOTION

In today's world of constant noise—phones buzzing, schedules packed, and media distracting—many believers have lost the art of the secret place. We give God leftovers instead of first fruits. We seek His blessing without seeking His face.

But stewardship of much requires discipline of much. Leaders, ministers, parents, and workers cannot fulfill their responsibilities apart from prayer and fasting. Our strength will fail if our secret life is empty.

PRACTICAL STEPS FOR A STRONG SECRET LIFE

1. **Set a daily appointment with God** – Treat prayer like a non-negotiable meeting.

2. **Incorporate fasting regularly** – Begin with one meal or a day, and grow into extended fasts as God leads.

3. **Guard against distraction** – Put away devices, silence noise, and focus wholly on God.

4. **Keep a prayer journal** – Record prayers, answers, and revelations to track your spiritual stewardship.

REFLECTION

1. How consistent is your secret life of prayer and fasting?

2. Are you more devoted to public ministry or private intimacy with God?

3. What distractions do you need to remove in order to strengthen your secret place?

PRAYER

Father, I thank You for the privilege of intimacy with You. Forgive me for the times I have neglected prayer or resisted fasting. Teach me to value the secret place above public recognition. Please help me to discipline my flesh so that my spirit may be strengthened. Let my hidden life with You be the foundation of everything I do in public. May prayer and fasting become my delight, not my burden. And may my secret devotion bring You glory openly. In Jesus' name. Amen.

Chapter 8

Guarding the Heart in Times of Abundance

THE TEST OF PROSPERITY

Many believers think the greatest test of faith is hardship, but scripture shows that prosperity can be even more dangerous. When we have little, we cling to God in desperation. But when we abound, the temptation is to forget Him.

Deuteronomy 8:10–14 gives this warning:

> **"When you have eaten and are full, then you shall bless the Lord your God for the good land which He has given you. "Beware that you do not forget the Lord your God by not keeping His commandments, His judgments, and His statutes which I command you today, lest—when you have eaten and are full, and have built beautiful houses and dwell in them; and when your herds and your flocks multiply, and your silver and your gold are multiplied, and all that you have is multiplied; when your heart is lifted up, and you forget the Lord your God who brought you out of the land of Egypt, from the house of bondage;"**

Abundance is not evil, but it is dangerous. It tests humility, dependence, and gratitude.

THE SUBTLE DANGERS OF ABUNDANCE

1. Pride – Believing success is self-made rather than God-given (**see Daniel 4:30**).

2. Forgetfulness – Losing sight of the God who provided.

3. Complacency – Becoming spiritually lazy because life feels secure.

4. Idolatry – Trusting in wealth, influence, or resources instead of God (**see 1 Timothy 6:17**).

The higher God lifts us, the more fiercely the enemy seeks to corrupt our hearts.

BIBLICAL EXAMPLES

- Solomon began with wisdom, humility, and devotion, but abundance led him into compromise and idolatry (**see 1 Kings 11:1–4**).

- Hezekiah was blessed with prosperity, yet pride after his healing brought judgment (**see 2 Chronicles 32:25–26**).

- The Laodicean Church said, **"I am rich, and increased with goods, and have need of nothing"**—yet Jesus called them wretched and blind (**see Revelation 3:17**).

Each example shows how abundance can slowly erode devotion if the heart is not guarded.

GUARDING THE HEART IN SEASONS OF PLENTY

Proverbs 4:23 instructs: **"Keep your heart with all diligence, for out of it spring the issues of life." (NKJV).** Guarding the heart in abundance requires intentional practices:

1. **Gratitude** – Consistently acknowledging God as the source of all blessings.

2. **Generosity** – Giving freely to keep greed from taking root.

3. **Humility** – Remembering we are stewards, not owners.

4. **Discipline** – Continuing prayer, fasting, and holiness, even when life feels easy.

Abundance should deepen our worship, not diminish it.

JESUS' WARNING ABOUT RICHES

Jesus often warned about the deceitfulness of riches. In Matthew 19:23, He said: **"Assuredly, I say to you that it is hard for a rich man to enter the kingdom of heaven." (NKJV).**

This was not because riches themselves condemn, but because riches tempt the heart toward independence. The danger of abundance is that we may no longer feel desperate for God. But when wealth and prosperity are surrendered to Christ, they become powerful tools for kingdom expansion.

MODERN APPLICATION

- A business owner must guard against pride, remembering that their success is from God.

- A believer blessed financially must resist greed by practicing generosity and tithing.

- A leader with influence must avoid self-glory, keeping Christ at the center.

- Families living in comfort must guard against complacency by maintaining spiritual disciplines.

Abundance is not proof of favor, unless it is stewarded faithfully.

THE TRUE MEASURE OF ABUNDANCE

True abundance is not how much we possess but how much we can release for God's purposes. The believer who guards their heart in plenty will find that prosperity does not destroy them—it strengthens their testimony.

Paul declared in Philippians 4:12, **"I know how to be abased, and I know how to abound." (NKJV).** Both require discipline. Both require grace. Both require stewardship.

REFLECTION

1. How do you respond differently to God in seasons of lack versus seasons of abundance?

2. Are you more tempted to forget God when life feels comfortable?

3. What practices of gratitude, generosity, and humility can you strengthen to guard your heart?

PRAYER

Father, I thank You for every blessing and provision You have given me. I acknowledge that all good things come from You. Forgive me for the times I have allowed abundance to dull my devotion. Teach me to guard my heart with humility, gratitude, and generosity. Keep me dependent on You, whether in lack or plenty. May my life always testify that You, not my possessions, are my source and security. Help me to steward abundance with integrity so that You are glorified in all things. In Jesus' name. Amen.

Part III

Responsibility in Ministry and Leadership

Chapter 9

Shepherds of God's Flock

THE WEIGHT OF SHEPHERDING

L eadership in God's kingdom is not a position of privilege but a place of responsibility. The prophet Ezekiel delivered a sharp rebuke to unfaithful shepherds: **"Woe to the shepherds of Israel who feed themselves! Should not the shepherds feed the flocks?" (Ezekiel 34:2 - NKJV).** God holds shepherds accountable, not just for their own lives but for the lives of those entrusted to their care.

Pastoral ministry is not about titles, stages, or applause — it is about feeding, guiding, protecting, and nurturing God's sheep. Hebrews 13:17 warns that leaders will give an account: **"Obey those who rule over you, and be submissive, for they watch out for your souls, as those who must give account." (NKJV).**

THE SHEPHERD'S MANDATE

A shepherd's responsibilities mirror those of Christ, the Chief Shepherd:

1. **Feed the flock** – Provide sound doctrine and spiritual nourishment (**see John 21:15–17**).

2. **Protect the flock** – Guard against false teachers, deception, and danger (**see Acts 20:28–29**).

3. **Guide the flock** – Lead with wisdom and integrity, not domination (**see 1 Peter 5:2–3**).

4. **Care for the wounded** – Bind up the brokenhearted and restore the fallen (**see Ezekiel 34:4**).

Leadership is measured not by how many follow, but by how faithfully one serves.

THE DANGER OF NEGLIGENT SHEPHERDS

Scripture repeatedly warns of irresponsible leadership:

- Hirelings flee when wolves come (**see John 10:12–13**).

- False shepherds exploit the flock for gain (**see Jeremiah 23:1–2**).

- Prideful leaders exalt themselves instead of Christ (**see 3 John 9–10**).

When shepherds fail, sheep scatter. But when shepherds lead with love, sheep flourish.

THE EXAMPLE OF THE GOOD SHEPHERD

Jesus called Himself the Good Shepherd who **"giveth His life for the sheep" (see John 10:11).** His model of leadership was sacrificial, compassionate, and servant-hearted. True shepherds must reflect His character, putting the needs of the sheep above their own comfort or recognition.

MODERN APPLICATION

- A pastor diligently studies scripture to feed the congregation sound doctrine rather than chasing trends.

- A ministry leader protects new believers from harmful influences by teaching discernment.

- A mentor invests time in discipling others, not for recognition but for their growth.

- A church leader sacrifices personal convenience to serve faithfully.

God's flock requires shepherds who love enough to lead and lead enough to love.

THE REWARD OF FAITHFUL SHEPHERDS

1 Peter 5:4 promises: **"and when the Chief Shepherd appears, you will receive the crown of glory that does not fade away."**

(NKJV). Faithful shepherds may be unrecognized by men, but they are honored by God.

Every sermon preached, prayer prayed, and soul nurtured is noticed by the Chief Shepherd. Leadership stewardship will be rewarded eternally.

REFLECTION

1. Are you leading for recognition, or out of love for God's flock?

2. Do you see leadership as a privilege or as a weight of responsibility?

3. How can you reflect Christ, the Good Shepherd, more in your ministry or service?

PRAYER

Lord, thank You for entrusting me with influence in the lives of others. Forgive me for the times I have led carelessly or selfishly. Teach me to shepherd with Your heart—feeding faithfully, guiding wisely, protecting diligently, and loving sacrificially. May my leadership point others to You, the Chief Shepherd. And may I one day receive the crown of glory as a faithful steward of Your flock. In Jesus' name. Amen.

Chapter 10

Leadership Without Compromise

THE PRESSURE LEADERS FACE

Leadership in God's kingdom is not for the faint-hearted. Leaders face pressure from culture, expectations from people, and temptations from the enemy. Compromise often looks like the easier path—pleasing men instead of God, softening truth to avoid offense, or cutting corners to maintain comfort.

But scripture warns: **"The fear of man brings a snare, but whoever trusts in the Lord shall be safe." (Proverbs 29:25 - NKJV).** Leaders who compromise to appease people eventually lose both credibility and effectiveness.

THE CALL TO STAND FIRM

Paul exhorted Timothy: **"Preach the word! Be ready in season and out of season. Convince, rebuke, exhort, with all longsuffering and teaching." (2 Timothy 4:2 - NKJV).** In other words, proclaim truth when it's popular and when it's not.

True leadership requires:

1. **Conviction** – Standing on biblical truth regardless of shifting culture.

2. **Courage** – Refusing to bow to pressure or fear.

3. **Consistency** – Living what you preach, even when no one is watching.

4. **Character** – Valuing holiness above charisma.

BIBLICAL EXAMPLES OF UNCOMPROMISING LEADERSHIP

- Daniel refused to defile himself with the king's food (**see Daniel 1:8**). His conviction opened doors for promotion and influence.

- Shadrach, Meshach, and Abednego refused to bow to the golden image, even at the threat of death (**see Daniel 3:16–18**). Their stand revealed God's power.

- Peter and John boldly declared before the Sanhedrin, **"We ought to obey God rather than men" (Acts 5:29 - NKJV).**

- Paul declared, **"none of these things move me; nor do I count my life dear to myself, so that I may finish my race with joy, and the ministry which I received from the Lord Jesus, to testify to the gospel of the grace of God." (Acts 20:24 - NKJV).**

Each leader faced pressure to compromise but chose obedience to God above all.

THE COST OF COMPROMISE

Compromise often begins small but grows destructive.

- Saul compromised by sparing King Agag and the best of the Amalekite spoil (**see 1 Samuel 15:9–11**). His disobedience cost him the throne.

- Samson compromised by revealing his secret to Delilah (**see Judges 16:17–20**). His strength and vision were lost.

- Many priests in Malachi's day compromised worship, offering polluted sacrifices (**see Malachi 1:7–8**). God rejected their service.

Compromise always brings loss—of power, anointing, credibility, and ultimately God's approval.

MODERN APPLICATION: LEADERS TODAY

- A pastor refusing to dilute biblical truth, even when culture resists.

- A business leader choosing honesty over profit.

- A parent leading children in righteousness, even when the world promotes ungodliness.

- A young leader refusing to build ministry on trends instead of truth.

The uncompromising leader may not be applauded by the world, but they will be honored by God.

THE REWARD OF INTEGRITY

Psalm 25:21 declares: **"Let integrity and uprightness preserve me, for I wait for You." (NKJV).** Integrity preserves. Compromise destroys. Faithful leaders who stand firm will hear the words every steward longs for: **"Well done, thou good and faithful servant."**

REFLECTION

1. Where are you tempted to compromise in leadership?

2. Do you value people's approval more than God's approval?

3. What conviction must you strengthen to remain faithful?

PRAYER

Lord, strengthen me to lead without compromise. Forgive me for the times I have bent to pressure or sought the approval of men over You. Please give me the courage to stand firm, the conviction to uphold the truth, and the consistency to live what I preach. May my leadership be marked by integrity and holiness, and may my life point others to Christ, who is the ultimate standard of uncompromising leadership. In Jesus' name. Amen.

Chapter 11

Accountability in Leadership

THE PRINCIPLE OF LEADERSHIP ACCOUNTABILITY

L eadership in the kingdom is never independent; it is always accountable. Hebrews 13:17 says: **"Obey those who rule over you, and be submissive, for they watch out for your souls, as those who must give account. Let them do so with joy and not with grief, for that would be unprofitable for you."** **(NKJV).**

This means leaders will one day stand before God, not only for their own lives but also for the lives of those they led. The greater the influence, the greater the accountability. To whom much is given in leadership, much is required in responsibility.

BIBLICAL MODELS OF ACCOUNTABILITY

- Moses carried the weight of Israel's disobedience, interceding for them even when they rebelled (**see Exodus 32:11–14**).

- Eli was judged severely because he failed to correct his sons, though he was responsible as priest and father (**see 1 Samuel 3:13**).

- David was held accountable for numbering Israel, and judgment came upon the people (**see 2 Samuel 24:10–15**).

- Paul constantly reminded churches of his accountability before God, living transparently and urging them to imitate his example (**see 1 Corinthians 11:1**).

Each example reveals this truth: *leadership multiplies accountability.*

THE AREAS OF LEADERSHIP ACCOUNTABILITY

1. **Doctrinal Accountability** – Leaders must guard truth and teach sound doctrine (**see Titus 1:9**). Leading people astray brings severe judgment (**see James 3:1**).

2. **Moral Accountability** – Leaders must live holy lives, free from corruption, greed, and hypocrisy (**see 1 Timothy 3:2–7**). Their example influences the entire flock.

3. **Stewardship Accountability** – Leaders are entrusted with people, resources, and opportunities. They must steward these faithfully, not wastefully (**see Luke 16:2**).

4. **Relational Accountability** – Leaders must not abuse authority but lead with humility, compassion, and servant-heartedness **(see Mark 10:42–45)**.

THE BLESSING OF ACCOUNTABILITY

Accountability is not meant to be a burden but a safeguard. Leaders who embrace accountability:

- Remain humble, knowing they are not above correction.
- Stay aligned with God's will, avoiding pride and error.
- Inspire trust, because people see integrity and transparency.

Proverbs 27:17 says, **"As iron sharpens iron, so a man sharpens the countenance of his friend." (NKJV).** Leaders thrive when they remain accountable to God and to others.

THE DANGER OF REJECTING ACCOUNTABILITY

Many leaders fall when they believe they are untouchable. Pride whispers: *"No one can correct me. I answer to no one."* But isolation leads to destruction.

- King Saul rejected Samuel's correction, and God rejected him from being king **(see 1 Samuel 15:23)**.

- Uzziah ignored priestly rebuke and entered the temple in pride—God struck him with leprosy **(see 2 Chronicles 26:16–20)**.

A leader without accountability becomes dangerous to themselves and to others.

MODERN APPLICATION

- Pastors must remain accountable in doctrine and finances.

- Leaders must open themselves to mentors and peers for correction.

- Parents must model accountability at home, teaching children responsibility.

- Christian professionals must hold to integrity, even when no one is watching.

Leadership without accountability is leadership headed toward collapse.

THE ULTIMATE ACCOUNTABILITY

2 Corinthians 5:10 reminds us: **"For we must all appear before the judgment seat of Christ, that each one may receive the things done in the body, according to what he has done, whether good or bad." (NKJV).** Every leader will stand before God. Titles will not matter; faithfulness will. Crowds may applaud, but heaven's evaluation will be final.

Faithful leaders long to hear: **"Well done, good and faithful servant" (see Matthew 25:23).** That is the true reward of accountable leadership.

REFLECTION

1. Do you have people in your life who can hold you accountable?

2. Are you leading with transparency in doctrine, morality, and stewardship?

3. How would your leadership change if you lived daily with the awareness that you must give account before God?

PRAYER

Lord, thank You for entrusting me with influence. I recognize that with leadership comes accountability. Forgive me for any time I have resisted correction or ignored responsibility. Keep me humble, teachable, and faithful in every area of stewardship. Place mentors, peers, and voices of wisdom around me to sharpen me. Above all, prepare me to stand before You with joy, knowing I led with integrity and obedience. In Jesus' name. Amen.

Chapter 12

Servant Leadership: The Model of Christ

THE INVERTED KINGDOM MODEL

In the world, leadership is often measured by power, status, and authority. But Jesus inverted the model. In Matthew 20:26–28 He declared: **"whoever desires to become great among you, let him be your servant. And whoever desires to be first among you, let him be your slave—just as the Son of Man did not come to be served, but to serve, and to give His life a ransom for many." (NKJV).**

True kingdom leadership is not about climbing higher but stooping lower. Greatness in God's kingdom is measured by service.

JESUS: THE ULTIMATE SERVANT LEADER

Jesus, the eternal Son of God, humbled Himself to serve. Philippians 2:6–7 tells us that He **"made Himself of no reputation, taking the form of a bondservant, and coming in the likeness of men." (NKJV).**

- He washed His disciples' feet (**see John 13:14–15**).

- He touched lepers when others avoided them.

- He fed the hungry, healed the sick, and comforted the broken.

- He laid down His life as the ultimate act of servant leadership.

The cross was not just redemption—it was leadership through sacrifice.

THE MARKS OF SERVANT LEADERSHIP

1. **Humility** – Servant leaders do not seek titles, applause, or recognition. They seek to glorify Christ.

2. **Compassion** – They are moved by the needs of others, not self-interest.

3. **Sacrifice** – They are willing to give time, resources, and comfort for the sake of others.

4. **Integrity** – They lead by example, not by demand.

5. **Empowerment** – They raise others up instead of keeping them down.

THE CONTRAST WITH WORLDLY LEADERSHIP

Worldly leadership says, "Serve me."

Servant leadership says, "I will serve you."

Worldly leadership seeks control.

Servant leadership seeks influence through love and example.

Worldly leadership pursues position.

Servant leadership embraces responsibility.

This is why servant leadership has eternal weight—it reflects the very heart of Christ.

BIBLICAL EXAMPLES OF SERVANT LEADERSHIP

- Moses interceded for Israel, even offering to be blotted out of God's book for their sake (**see Exodus 32:32**).

- Nehemiah rebuilt Jerusalem's walls, not from a palace but by laboring among the people (**see Nehemiah 4:21–23**).

- Paul poured himself out like a drink offering for the churches he planted (**see Philippians 2:17**).

These leaders were remembered not for titles, but for sacrifice.

MODERN APPLICATION

- A pastor caring for the sick and visiting homes, not just preaching from the pulpit.

- A leader mentoring others rather than competing with them.

- A Christian professional using influence to serve employees and clients with dignity.

- Parents leading their homes by example, showing love and sacrifice daily.

Servant leadership transforms families, churches, and communities because it reflects the heart of Christ.

THE REWARD OF SERVANT LEADERS

Jesus promised in John 12:26: **"If anyone serves Me, let him follow Me; and where I am, there My servant will be also. If anyone serves Me, him My Father will honor." (NKJV).**

The world may overlook servant leaders, but the Father honors them. Their reward is eternal, and their legacy lives on in the lives they touched.

REFLECTION

1. Do you view leadership as a privilege to be served, or as a responsibility to serve?

2. How can you intentionally practice servant leadership in your home, church, or workplace?

3. In what ways can you reflect Christ's humility in your leadership role?

PRAYER

Lord Jesus, thank You for showing me the true model of leadership. You, the King of kings, humbled Yourself to serve and gave Your life as a ransom for many. Forgive me for the times I have desired position more than service, or recognition more than responsibility. Teach me to lead like You—with humility, compassion, sacrifice, and integrity. Help me to raise others up and to glorify You in all that I do. May I be found faithful as a servant leader in Your kingdom. In Your name. Amen.

Part IV

Stewardship in the World

Chapter 13

Managing Finances God's Way

THE TEST OF MONEY

Jesus spoke more about money than almost any other subject. Why? Because money reveals the heart. In Matthew 6:21 He said: **"For where your treasure is, there your heart will be also." (NKJV).**

Finances are not neutral—they are spiritual indicators. To whom much is given financially, much is required in stewardship. God is less interested in the amount we possess and more concerned with how we manage it.

OWNERSHIP VS. STEWARDSHIP

Psalm 24:1 declares: **"The earth is the Lord's, and all its fullness, the world and those who dwell therein." (NKJV).** Everything belongs to God. We are not owners; we are managers.

This mindset shifts how we handle resources:

- Owners ask: *"What do I want to do with my money?"*

- Stewards ask: *"Lord, how do You want me to use what You've entrusted to me?"*

BIBLICAL PRINCIPLES OF FINANCIAL STEWARDSHIP

1. **Tithing** – Returning the first tenth to God (**see Malachi 3:10**). It acknowledges His ownership and invites His blessing.

2. **Generosity** – Giving beyond tithes to bless others and advance the kingdom (**see 2 Corinthians 9:6–7**).

3. **Avoiding Debt** – Proverbs 22:7 warns: **"the borrower is servant to the lender." (NKJV).** Wise stewardship avoids unnecessary bondage.

4. **Planning and Saving** – Joseph stored grain in Egypt, preparing for famine (**see Genesis 41:48–49**). Wise saving honors God.

5. **Contentment** – Hebrews 13:5 says: **"Let your conduct be without covetousness; be content with such things as you have." (NKJV).**

THE DANGER OF LOVING MONEY

1 Timothy 6:10 warns: **"For the love of money is a root of all kinds of evil." (NKJV).** Money itself is not evil, but when it becomes an idol, it destroys. Many ruin ministries, families, and

faith by chasing wealth. Jesus warned that we cannot serve both God and mammon (**see Matthew 6:24**).

- Money can buy comfort but not peace.
- Money can build houses but not homes.
- Money can purchase influence but not integrity.

The true measure of wealth is eternal fruit, not earthly riches.

BIBLICAL EXAMPLES

- Abraham was blessed with riches but lived as a pilgrim, trusting God, not possessions (**see Genesis 13:2–4**).

- Job lost everything yet remained faithful, proving his devotion was not tied to wealth (**see Job 1:21**).

- The rich young ruler walked away from Jesus because he loved possessions more than eternal life (**see Mark 10:21–22**).

- The widow gave two mites—all she had—and Jesus declared her offering greater than the rich (**see Mark 12:43–44**).

MODERN APPLICATION

- A believer faithfully tithing, even when bills are tight, demonstrating trust in God's provision.

- A Christian business owner reinvesting profits into missions and ministry.

- A family living below their means to remain debt-free and generous.

- A young professional practicing financial discipline to avoid the trap of materialism.

When finances are surrendered to God, they become tools for kingdom expansion, not stumbling blocks of greed.

THE REWARD OF FAITHFUL FINANCIAL STEWARDSHIP

Luke 16:11 says: **"Therefore if you have not been faithful in the unrighteous mammon, who will commit to your trust the true riches?" (NKJV).** Faithfulness with money opens the door to spiritual trust. God uses finances as a training ground for greater responsibility.

Proverbs 11:25 promises: **"The generous soul will be made rich, and he who waters will also be watered himself." (NKJV).** Generosity always multiplies blessings.

REFLECTION

1. Do you see yourself as the owner of your money or the steward of God's resources?

2. Are you faithfully tithing, giving, saving, and living with contentment?

3. What financial habits need surrender so that you honor God with your resources?

PRAYER

Lord, thank You for every resource You have entrusted to me. I confess that all I have belongs to You. Forgive me for the times I have mismanaged money or loved possessions more than Your presence. Teach me to tithe faithfully, give generously, save wisely, and live contentedly. May my finances serve Your kingdom, not my greed. Please help me to be a faithful steward, so I may be entrusted with true riches. In Jesus' name. Amen.

Chapter 14

Time, Talent, and Treasure

THE THREEFOLD TRUST

God has given every believer three universal resources: *time, talent, and treasure.* Each is a gift, and each carries responsibility. Together, they represent the sum of our stewardship.

- Time is the most limited—it cannot be regained once lost.

- Talent is unique—it reflects our individual design and calling.

- Treasure is tangible—it represents our material and financial resources.

To whom much is given in any of these areas, much is required. Faithfulness demands that we invest all three for God's glory.

TIME: THE UNRENEWABLE RESOURCE

Ephesians 5:15–16 exhorts: **"See then that you walk circumspectly, not as fools but as wise, redeeming the time, because the days are evil." (NKJV).**

Time is life's most precious currency. Unlike money, it cannot be saved, multiplied, or recovered. Every day is a gift from God that must be invested wisely.

Dangers of Poor Time Stewardship:

1. **Procrastination** – Delaying obedience or kingdom work.

2. **Distraction** – Wasting hours on meaningless pursuits.

3. **Busyness without fruitfulness** – Filling schedules but neglecting purpose.

BIBLICAL EXAMPLES

- Noah used his time to obey God and build the ark (**see Genesis 6:22**).

- The five wise virgins prepared with oil while the foolish wasted time (**see Matthew 25:1–13**).

- Jesus fulfilled His mission in just over three years, proving the power of focused time stewardship (**see John 9:4**).

PRACTICAL STEWARDSHIP OF TIME

- Start each day with prayer and purpose.
- Prioritize eternal things over temporary distractions.
- Create rhythms of rest and renewal, not just activity.

TALENT: THE GOD-GIVEN ABILITY

1 Peter 4:10 declares: **"As each one has received a gift, minister it to one another, as good stewards of the manifold grace of God." (NKJV).**

Every believer has gifts—spiritual and natural. Talents are entrusted, not for selfish ambition but for service.

The Parable of the Talents (see Matthew 25:14–30):

- The faithful servants multiplied what they were given.

- The unfaithful servant buried his gift out of fear and laziness.

- The master rewarded fruitfulness and condemned unfaithfulness.

LESSONS

- God expects multiplication, not stagnation.
- Excuses are not acceptable stewardship.
- Faithful use of small talents leads to greater trust.

Dangers of Misusing Talent:

1. **Neglect** – Refusing to develop or use gifts.

2. **Pride** – Using talents for self-glory rather than God's.

3. **Comparison** – Coveting others' talents instead of maximizing our own.

Practical Stewardship of Talent:

1. Discover your gifts through prayer, service, and feedback.
2. Develop your skills with discipline and diligence.
3. Deploy your talents in the body of Christ and in the world.

TREASURE: THE MATERIAL RESOURCE

Jesus said in Matthew 6:19–20: **"Do not lay up for yourselves treasures on earth, where moth and rust destroy and where thieves break in and steal; but lay up for yourselves treasures in heaven, where neither moth nor rust destroys and where thieves do not break in and steal." (NKJV).** Treasure includes finances, possessions, and material wealth.

God entrusts resources to us, not just for survival but for service.

The Dangers of Misusing Treasure:

1. **Greed** – Hoarding instead of sharing.
2. **Covetousness** – Always craving more without gratitude.
3. **Wastefulness** – Spending without kingdom purpose.

Examples of Stewardship:

- The early church sold possessions to meet needs (**see Acts 4:34–35**).

- The Macedonians gave generously out of poverty (**see 2 Corinthians 8:2–3**).

- The poor widow gave her last two mites, and Jesus honored her sacrifice (**see Mark 12:43–44**).

Practical Stewardship of Treasure:

- Tithe faithfully to honor God.

- Give generously to bless others.

- Budget wisely to avoid waste and debt.

- Invest resources into eternal impact, not just temporal comfort.

THE INTERCONNECTION OF TIME, TALENT, AND TREASURE

These three trusts are not separate—they work together.

- Time is used to develop talent.

- Talent can produce treasure.

- Treasure can buy more effective use of time and talent for the kingdom.

For example, a believer uses time to study, develops teaching talent, and invests treasure to write a book that reaches thousands for Christ. When all three are stewarded together, kingdom impact multiplies.

THE ETERNAL PERSPECTIVE

Paul reminds us in 2 Corinthians 5:10: **"For we must all appear before the judgment seat of Christ…" (NKJV).** Our use of time, talent, and treasure will be tested. Did we waste them on ourselves, or invest them for eternity?

The faithful steward will hear: **"Well done, good and faithful servant" (see Matthew 25:23).**

REFLECTION

1. How are you spending your time—on eternal pursuits or empty distractions?

2. Are you fully using your God-given talents to serve others and glorify Him?

3. Do you view your treasure as yours to own or God's to steward?

4. Which of these three areas needs the most realignment in your life?

PRAYER

Lord, I acknowledge that my time, talents, and treasure all belong to You. Forgive me for wasted hours, neglected gifts, or misused resources. Teach me to redeem the time, to multiply my talents, and to invest my treasure wisely. Help me to live with eternity in view, knowing that I will give an account of all You have entrusted to me. May my life be a testimony of faithful stewardship in every area. In Jesus' name. Amen.

Chapter 15

Serving Others with Compassion and Sacrifice

THE CALL TO SERVE

Jesus said in Mark 10:45: **"For even the Son of Man did not come to be served, but to serve, and to give His life a ransom for many." (NKJV).**

If Christ, the Lord of glory, came to serve, then all who follow Him must live as servants. Stewardship is not just about managing money or gifts—it is about how we use those resources to bless others. To whom much is given, much is required in compassion and sacrificial service.

COMPASSION: THE HEART OF SERVICE

Compassion is love in action. It is not pity, but power released through love. Scripture often says of Jesus: **"He was moved with compassion" (see Matthew 9:36; 14:14).** Compassion stirred Him to heal the sick, feed the hungry, and teach the lost.

True stewardship of compassion involves:

1. **Seeing needs clearly** – Not turning away from suffering.

2. **Feeling deeply** – Allowing God's love to stir our hearts.

3. **Acting sacrificially** – Doing something tangible to meet the need.

Compassion without action is sentiment. Compassion with sacrifice is stewardship.

THE SACRIFICE OF SERVICE

Serving others often requires giving up comfort, convenience, and recognition. Paul wrote in Philippians 2:17: **"Yes, and if I am being poured out as a drink offering on the sacrifice and service of your faith, I am glad and rejoice with you all." (NKJV).**

Sacrifice in service may mean:

- Time spent helping the needy instead of pursuing personal leisure.

- Giving resources that stretch us beyond convenience.

- Enduring inconvenience or even rejection while serving others.

The good Samaritan (**see Luke 10:30–37**) is a model of sacrificial service. He stopped, cared for a stranger, spent his money, and ensured continued care—all while others walked by.

BIBLICAL EXAMPLES OF COMPASSIONATE SERVICE

- Dorcas (Tabitha) made clothes for widows, and her compassion left such an impact that Peter raised her from the dead (**see Acts 9:36–41**).

- Barnabas sold land to support the early church and lived as an encourager to new believers (**see Acts 4:36–37**).

- Jesus fed thousands with loaves and fish because He would not send them away hungry (**see Mark 8:2**).

These lives prove that service is remembered in eternity, even if unnoticed on earth.

MODERN APPLICATION

- Churches feeding the hungry and clothing the poor in their communities.

- Believers volunteering time to mentor youth or serve in missions.

- Families opening their homes to those in need of hospitality.

- Christians giving sacrificially to support kingdom work around the globe.

True greatness is not in being served, but in serving.

THE REWARD OF COMPASSIONATE SACRIFICE

Jesus promised in Matthew 25:40: **"Assuredly, I say to you, inasmuch as you did it to one of the least of these My brethren, you did it to Me." (NKJV).** Every act of service to others is service to Christ Himself.

Though service often goes unnoticed by men, it is seen and rewarded by God. Eternal crowns await those who pour out their lives for others **(see 2 Timothy 4:7–8)**.

REFLECTION

1. When was the last time you served someone without expecting recognition?

2. Do you see service as a burden or as a privilege?

3. What sacrifices can you make to show compassion in practical ways this week?

PRAYER

Lord, thank You for serving me through the sacrifice of the cross. Fill me with Your compassion so that I may see and respond to the needs around me. Forgive me for the times I have chosen comfort over sacrifice. Teach me to serve with joy, humility, and love, even when no one notices. May every act of service point others to You and bring glory to Your name. In Jesus' name. Amen.

Chapter 16

Responsibility to the Poor, the Lost, and the Least

THE CALL TO HOLISTIC STEWARDSHIP

S tewardship is never self-contained. God entrusts us with resources, not simply for personal growth or ministry advancement but to meet the needs of the poor, to reach the lost, and to care for the least among us. Jesus summarized this heart in Matthew 25:40:

> **"Assuredly, I say to you, inasmuch as you did it to one of the least of these My brethren, you did it to Me." (NKJV).**

Every act of compassion, every effort in evangelism, and every defense of the vulnerable is a direct service to Christ.

RESPONSIBILITY TO THE POOR

Scripture consistently emphasizes God's concern for the poor:

- "He who has pity on the poor lends to the Lord, and He will pay back what he has given." (Proverbs 19:17 - NKJV).

- Jesus said: **"For you have the poor with you always..."** (Mark 14:7 - NKJV).

- James warned that true religion includes caring for the fatherless and widows (see James 1:27).

Stewardship of the poor means more than occasional charity. It requires sustained responsibility—advocacy, generosity, and justice.

Biblical examples:

1. Ruth was sustained by gleaning because God commanded landowners to leave portions for the poor (see Leviticus 19:9–10).

2. The early church ensured no believer lacked, selling possessions to meet needs (see Acts 4:34–35).

Faithful stewardship demands that we share abundance rather than hoard it.

RESPONSIBILITY TO THE LOST

The great commission is the highest stewardship: **"Go into all the world and preach the gospel to every creature." (Mark 16:15 - NKJV).** Souls are more valuable than silver and gold.

To whom much is given in salvation, much is required in evangelism. We cannot keep the gospel to ourselves. Paul said in Romans 1:14: **"I am a debtor both to Greeks and to barbarians, both to wise and to unwise." (NKJV).**

The lost are our responsibility because:

1. Christ died for all.
2. We have the message of reconciliation.
3. Eternity is at stake.

Neglecting the lost is poor stewardship of the greatest treasure ever given—the gospel.

RESPONSIBILITY TO THE LEAST

The "least" refers to those overlooked, marginalized, or powerless in society. Jesus often elevated the least:

- He touched lepers.
- He welcomed children.
- He dined with outcasts and sinners.

Kingdom stewardship includes lifting those the world despises. Philippians 2:4 commands: **"Let each of you look out not only for his own interests, but also for the interests of others." (NKJV).**

To ignore the least is to misrepresent Christ, who Himself became lowly for our sake.

MODERN APPLICATION

- Supporting missions and outreach to bring the gospel to unreached people.

- Feeding the hungry, housing the homeless, and clothing the needy.

- Mentoring at-risk youth, defending the unborn, and visiting prisoners.

- Welcoming immigrants, refugees, and those society forgets.

When we serve the poor, the lost, and the least, we reflect the kingdom's heart.

THE ETERNAL ACCOUNTABILITY

Matthew 25:31–46 gives the sobering parable of the sheep and the goats. The distinction was not between those who prayed or attended church but those who fed the hungry, clothed the naked, visited the imprisoned, and welcomed the stranger. Jesus' words are piercing: **"inasmuch as you did not do it to one of the least of these, you did not do it to Me." (NKJV).**

On judgment day, stewardship will not only be measured by how we managed our money or developed our talents, but also by how we treated the poor, the lost, and the least.

REFLECTION

1. How are you stewarding God's resources to care for the poor?

2. Do you see evangelism as your personal responsibility, or do you leave it to others?

3. Who are the "least" around you that God is calling you to serve?

4. How will eternity measure the way you treated others?

PRAYER

Father, thank You for entrusting me with the gospel, with resources, and with opportunities to serve. Forgive me for the times I have ignored the poor, overlooked the lost, or dismissed the least. Fill my heart with compassion, courage, and obedience. Teach me to see people as You see them. May my stewardship extend beyond myself to those who need hope, healing, and salvation. Let me hear Your voice say, **"Well done,"** because I loved and served the least of these. In Jesus' name. Amen.

Part V

The Eternal Perspective of Stewardship

Chapter 17

The Judgment Seat of Christ

THE REALITY OF ETERNAL ACCOUNTABILITY

One day, every believer will stand before the Lord, not for condemnation, but for evaluation. Romans 14:10–12 declares: **"But why do you judge your brother? Or why do you show contempt for your brother? For we shall all stand before the judgment seat of Christ. For it is written: "As I live, says the Lord, every knee shall bow to Me, and every tongue shall confess to God." So then each of us shall give account of himself to God." (NKJV).**

The Judgment Seat of Christ (Bema seat) is not about salvation— that is settled through Christ's finished work. Instead, it is about stewardship. What did we do with what He entrusted to us?

This judgment will reveal whether our works were of eternal value or temporary vanity.

THE NATURE OF THE JUDGMENT SEAT

Paul explained in 2 Corinthians 5:10: **"For we must all appear before the judgment seat of Christ, that each one may receive** the things done in the body, according to what he has done, whether good or bad." (NKJV).

Key truths about this judgment:

1. **It is universal** – All believers must stand before Christ.

2. **It is personal** – "Every one" must give an account individually.

3. **It is revealing** – Motives, actions, and stewardship will be exposed.

4. **It is rewarding or regretting** – Faithful stewards receive honor; unfaithful stewards suffer loss (**see 1 Corinthians 3:13–15**).

THE TESTING OF WORKS

Paul described works being tested by fire: **"If anyone's work which he has built on it endures, he will receive a reward. If anyone's work is burned, he will suffer loss; but he himself will be saved, yet so as through fire." (1 Corinthians 3:14–15 - NKJV).**

- Works done in faith, love, and obedience endure.

- Works done in pride, selfishness, or for human applause burn away.

The test is not quantity but quality. God values faithfulness over fame, obedience over outcomes.

MOTIVES MATTER

At the Bema seat, God will not only examine what we did, but why we did it. 1 Corinthians 4:5 says the Lord will **"bring to light the hidden things of darkness and reveal the counsels of the hearts. Then each one's praise will come from God." (NKJV)**.

- Did we serve to be seen by men?
- Did we give for recognition or out of genuine love?
- Did we preach to exalt Christ or ourselves?

Motives often matter more than methods.

THE JOY OF FAITHFUL STEWARDSHIP

For faithful stewards, the judgment seat is not a place of fear but of joy. Jesus promised in Matthew 25:23: **"Well done, good and faithful servant; you have been faithful over a few things, I will make you ruler over many things. Enter into the joy of your lord." (NKJV)**.

To hear those words is the highest honor of eternity.

THE SORROW OF NEGLECT

Yet for others, there will be regret—not loss of salvation, but loss of reward. To have wasted time, buried talents, or misused treasures will be a painful revelation. The unfaithful servant in the parable of the talents (**see Matthew 25:30**) was called wicked and slothful, even though he preserved what was given.

God expects multiplication, not stagnation.

MODERN APPLICATION

The Judgment Seat of Christ should shape how we live daily.

- Leaders must shepherd with eternity in mind.

- Believers must give, serve, and evangelize as those who will one day give an account.

- Parents must raise children, not just for worldly success but for eternal impact.

Living with the Bema seat in view keeps us from compromise, complacency, and distraction.

REFLECTION

1. Do you live with an awareness that you will stand before Christ?

2. Are your motives pure, or are you seeking recognition from people?

3. If your works were tested by fire today, how much would remain?

PRAYER

Lord Jesus, I know I will one day stand before You to give an account of my life. Forgive me for wasted time, buried talents, and misused treasures. Teach me to live with eternity in view. Purify my motives so that everything I do flows from love for You. Help me to be a faithful steward, so that on that day, I may hear, "Well done, good and faithful servant." In Your name I pray. Amen.

Chapter 18

Rewards and Crowns

THE PROMISE OF REWARDS

God is not unjust to forget our labor (**see Hebrews 6:10**). Every act of service, every sacrifice made, every prayer prayed, every soul won—none of it is wasted. The Bible teaches that faithful stewardship will be rewarded in eternity.

Jesus Himself declared: **"And behold, I am coming quickly, and My reward is with Me, to give to every one according to his work." (Revelation 22:12 - NKJV).**

Rewards are not about salvation—that is by grace alone. Rewards are about stewardship—what we did with the salvation and resources entrusted to us.

THE PRINCIPLE OF REWARDS

1 Corinthians 3:14–15 teaches that some works endure and bring reward, while others are burned away.

- Works done in faith and obedience become eternal treasures.

- Works done in selfishness or pride are temporary and worthless.

God measures not simply what we accomplished, but how faithfully we obeyed.

THE CROWNS IN SCRIPTURE

The New Testament speaks of five crowns promised to faithful believers:

1. **The Incorruptible Crown** – For disciplined living (**see 1 Corinthians 9:25–27**).

    - Reward for those who master the flesh, run with endurance, and live with self-control.

    - Symbolizes victory over sin and perseverance in holiness.

2. **The Crown of Rejoicing** – For soul-winners (**see 1 Thessalonians 2:19–20**).

    - Given to those who invest in evangelism and discipleship.

    - Every soul brought to Christ is a jewel in this crown.

3. **The Crown of Righteousness** – For those who love Christ's appearing (**see 2 Timothy 4:7–8**).

- Awarded to believers who live in readiness and expectation of Christ's return.

- Symbolizes devotion and longing for eternity with Him.

4. **The Crown of Life** – For those who endure trials and remain faithful unto death **(see James 1:12, Revelation 2:10)**.

   - Given to martyrs, persecuted believers, and all who withstand severe testing.

   - Represents triumph through suffering.

5. **The Crown of Glory** – For faithful shepherds and leaders **(see 1 Peter 5:2–4)**.

   - Awarded to pastors and leaders who guide God's flock with integrity and love.

   - Reflects the eternal honor for servant-hearted leadership.

THE PURPOSE OF REWARDS

Rewards are not for boasting in ourselves but for glorifying Christ. Revelation 4:11 pictures elders casting their crowns before the throne, declaring: **"You are worthy, O Lord, to receive glory and honor and power; for You created all things, and by Your will they [b]exist and were created." (NKJV).**

Every crown earned on earth will ultimately be laid at Jesus' feet. Our stewardship brings eternal worship.

THE LOSS OF REWARD

Scripture also warns of the possibility of loss. 2 John 8 cautions: **"Look to yourselves, that we do not lose those things we worked for, but that we may receive a full reward." (NKJV).**

- Disobedience can diminish reward.
- Neglect can waste opportunity.
- Compromise can forfeit eternal honor.

A believer may enter heaven saved, but empty-handed—saved **"so as by fire" (see 1 Corinthians 3:15).**

MODERN APPLICATION

- A believer who lives faithfully in obscurity may receive a greater reward than a famous preacher, because God measures faithfulness, not fame.

- A missionary who endures hardship with joy will wear the Crown of Life.

- A pastor who shepherds with humility will receive the Crown of Glory.

- An ordinary Christian who shares Christ at work will shine with the Crown of Rejoicing.

Eternal rewards are not for the spectacular but for the faithful.

LIVING FOR ETERNAL REWARD

Colossians 3:23–24 commands: **"And whatever you do, do it heartily, as to the Lord and not to men, knowing that from the Lord you will receive the reward of the inheritance; for you serve the Lord Christ." (NKJV).**

When we live with eternity in mind, every act—large or small—becomes an offering of stewardship that brings eternal reward.

REFLECTION

1. Are you living for earthly recognition or eternal reward?

2. Which crown are you most longing to receive, and are you living faithfully toward it?

3. Do you see your stewardship as temporary labor or as an eternal investment?

PRAYER

Lord, thank You that You are a just rewarder of those who diligently seek You. I long to live not for temporary applause but for eternal crowns. Purify my motives, strengthen my faithfulness, and keep my eyes fixed on Your coming. May every crown I receive be laid at Your feet in worship. In Jesus' name. Amen.

Chapter 19

Eternal Accountability for Earthly Responsibility

STEWARDSHIP HAS ETERNAL CONSEQUENCES

L ife on earth is a vapor (**see James 4:14**), but stewardship decisions made in this short life echo into eternity. What we do with time, talent, treasure, relationships, and opportunities will one day be weighed before the Lord.

Jesus' parables repeatedly stress accountability. In Matthew 25:19, after a long time, the master returned to settle accounts with his servants. Every steward had to give an answer for how he managed what was entrusted.

This is the sobering reality of stewardship: *temporary responsibility leads to eternal accountability.*

THE STANDARD OF ACCOUNTABILITY

God will not judge us by comparison with others but by the faithfulness of our own stewardship. Luke 12:48 declares: **"For** everyone to whom much is given, from him much will be required." (NKJV).

- Those given much in resources will answer for their generosity.

- Those given much in gifts will answer for their service.

- Those given much in leadership will answer for their influence.

- Those given much in revelation will answer for their obedience.

Every believer has been given something—and every believer will answer for it.

WHAT WILL BE EXAMINED?

At the judgment seat of Christ, God will examine:

1. **Our Works** – Did we build with gold and silver, or with wood and stubble? (**see 1 Corinthians 3:12–13**).

2. **Our Motives** – Did we serve out of love for Christ or out of pride and ambition? (**see 1 Corinthians 4:5**).

3. **Our Opportunities** – Did we make the most of every chance to advance God's kingdom? (**see Ephesians 5:16**).

4. **Our Faithfulness** – Did we endure trials, remain steadfast, and persevere to the end? (**see Matthew 24:13**).

Faithfulness, not fame, is the measure of eternal accountability.

THE JOY OF REWARDED STEWARDSHIP

For the faithful, accountability will be a moment of eternal joy. The Lord will say: **"Well done, good and faithful servant; you have been faithful over a few things, I will make you ruler over many things. Enter into the joy of your lord." (Matthew 25:23 - NKJV).**

This joy includes:

- The crown of life for endurance.
- The crown of righteousness for longing for Christ's return.
- The crown of rejoicing for soul-winning.
- The crown of glory for faithful shepherding.
- The incorruptible crown for disciplined perseverance.

Rewards are not merely symbolic—they represent eternal honor and responsibility in Christ's kingdom.

THE SORROW OF NEGLECTED STEWARDSHIP

For the unfaithful, accountability will bring loss, though not damnation. Paul said: **"he will suffer loss; but he himself will be saved, yet so as through fire." (1 Corinthians 3:15 - NKJV).**

Imagine standing before Christ with nothing to present—saved, but unfruitful. Eternal regret will mark those who squandered opportunities to live for God.

The parable of the unfaithful servant (**see Matthew 25:24–30**) reveals that burying gifts out of fear or laziness brings severe rebuke. God does not accept excuses where He expected fruitfulness.

MODERN APPLICATION

- A Christian who faithfully served in obscurity will be honored above those who sought fame.

- A parent who discipled children in Christ will be rewarded eternally for unseen faithfulness.

- A believer who gave sacrificially to missions will see eternal fruit from their generosity.

- A church that pursued comfort instead of souls may enter heaven with loss, having neglected the great commission.

Eternal accountability makes every small act significant.

LIVING WITH ETERNITY IN MIND

Paul said in 2 Corinthians 4:18: **"while we do not look at the things which are seen, but at the things which are not seen. For the things which are seen are temporary, but the things which are not seen are eternal." (NKJV).**

- Stewardship is temporary—heaven is eternal.
- Money fades—souls remain.
- Time passes—fruit endures.

- Titles vanish—faithfulness shines forever.

Living with eternity in mind transforms how we spend every day.

REFLECTION

1. Are you living with .a clear awareness of eternal accountability?

2. If Christ called you to give an account today, what would endure, and what would burn away?

3. Are you motivated more by earthly applause or eternal approval?

4. What changes must you make now to ensure faithfulness then?

PRAYER

Father, I recognize that life is short, but eternity is forever. Forgive me for living casually, as though stewardship did not matter. Please help me to live each day with eternity in mind. Strengthen me to be faithful in every responsibility, pure in every motive, and diligent in every opportunity. May I stand before You with joy, not regret, presenting a life well-stewarded for Your glory. In Jesus' name. Amen.

Part VI

Living with Purposeful Stewardship

Chapter 20

Living Ready: Anticipating Christ's Return

THE URGENCY OF READINESS

Stewardship is not an endless assignment—it has a deadline. Jesus Christ is coming again, and when He returns, every steward will give an account. Matthew 24:44 declares: **"Therefore you also be ready, for the Son of Man is coming at an hour you do not expect." (NKJV).**

The greatest motivation for stewardship is the imminent return of Christ. We do not know the day or hour, but we know the call: *live ready*.

THE PARABLE OF THE TEN VIRGINS

In Matthew 25:1–13, Jesus told of ten virgins waiting for the bridegroom:

- Five were wise and kept their lamps full of oil.

- Five were foolish and neglected their preparation.

When the bridegroom came, the wise entered in, but the foolish were shut out.

This parable teaches us that readiness cannot be borrowed or delayed. Stewardship requires daily faithfulness, not last-minute scrambling.

THE PARABLE OF THE FAITHFUL SERVANT

In Luke 12:42–46, Jesus described a faithful steward who watched and worked diligently while his master delayed. In contrast, the unfaithful steward grew careless, abusing others and wasting time. The faithful one was rewarded at the master's return; the unfaithful one faced severe judgment.

Faithful stewards live as though Christ could return today. Unfaithful stewards live as though He will never return.

SIGNS OF LIVING READY

1. **Holiness** – Keeping ourselves unspotted from the world (**see 2 Peter 3:11–12**).

2. **Faithfulness** – Using time, talent, and treasure consistently for the kingdom.

3. **Urgency** – Sharing the gospel with a lost world (**see Matthew 24:14**).

4. **Expectation** – Longing for Christ's appearing (**see 2 Timothy 4:8**).

Readiness is not fear-based; it is hope-filled. It is living with joyful anticipation that our King is near.

THE DANGER OF DELAY

Many live as though they have unlimited time, but Jesus warned against complacency: **"But if that servant says in his heart, 'My master is delaying his coming,' and begins to beat the male and female servants, and to eat and drink and be drunk, the master of that servant will come on a day when he is not looking for him, and at an hour when he is not aware, and will cut him in two and appoint him his portion with the unbelievers." (Luke 12:45–46 - NKJV).**

Spiritual procrastination is deadly. Stewardship wasted today cannot be recovered tomorrow.

MODERN APPLICATION

- A believer faithfully serving in the church, even when unnoticed, because they live for the Master's "Well done."

- A businessperson using influence for kingdom purposes instead of waiting until retirement.

- A student sharing the gospel with classmates now, not someday.

- Families living in daily devotion, training children in righteousness because Christ could come at any moment.

Living ready means aligning every area of life with eternity.

THE REWARD OF READINESS

Jesus promised in Luke 12:37: **"Blessed are those servants whom the master, when he comes, will find watching. Assuredly, I say to you that he will gird himself and have them sit down to eat, and will come and serve them." (NKJV).**

To live ready is to live blessed. The faithful steward will not be caught unprepared but will rejoice at His appearing.

REFLECTION

1. Are you living daily as though Christ could return at any moment?

2. What areas of your life show readiness, and what areas reveal neglect?

3. Who around you needs the gospel before it is too late?

4. If the Master returned today, would He find you faithful?

PRAYER

Lord Jesus, I believe You are coming again. Help me to live each day in readiness, not in fear but in joyful expectation. Forgive me for spiritual neglect and wasted opportunities. Teach me to keep my lamp burning with oil, my hands busy in service, and my heart steadfast in holiness. May I be found faithful when You return, prepared to enter into the joy of my Lord. Amen.

Chapter 21

Faithful to the End

THE RACE OF FAITH

The Christian life is often compared to a race. Hebrews 12:1–2 exhorts us: **"Therefore we also, since we are surrounded by so great a cloud of witnesses, let us lay aside every weight, and the sin which so easily ensnares us, and let us run with endurance the race that is set before us, looking unto Jesus, the author and finisher of our faith, who for the joy that was set before Him endured the cross, despising the shame, and has sat down at the right hand of the throne of God." (NKJV).**

In a race, it does not matter how quickly one starts if one fails to finish. Likewise, stewardship requires endurance, perseverance, and faithfulness until the end. Many begin with zeal, but only those who remain steadfast will receive the reward.

PAUL'S TESTIMONY OF FAITHFULNESS

Near the end of his life, Paul wrote with confidence: **"I have fought the good fight, I have finished the race, I have kept the faith." (2 Timothy 4:7 - NKJV).**

Paul's life was marked by:

- **Consistency** – Serving faithfully in hardship and abundance.

- **Resilience** – Remaining steadfast through persecution, imprisonment, and betrayal.

- **Focus** – Keeping his eyes fixed on the heavenly prize, not earthly gain.

His testimony reminds us that finishing well is the ultimate goal of stewardship.

THE DANGER OF FALLING AWAY

Scripture warns that some begin in faith but fall into neglect, compromise, or apostasy:

- Demas, who once labored with Paul, forsook him **"having loved this present world" (2 Timothy 4:10 - NKJV).**

- King Saul began with humility but ended in rebellion, rejected by God **(see 1 Samuel 15:23)**,

- Israel saw miracles in the wilderness but failed to enter the Promised Land due to unbelief **(see Hebrews 3:19)**.

Faithful stewardship is not measured at the beginning but at the finish line.

PERSEVERANCE IN TRIALS

Faithfulness is tested most severely in hardship. Jesus said in Matthew 24:13: **"But he who endures to the end shall be saved." (NKJV).**

- Trials refine stewardship.
- Suffering reveals loyalty.
- Opposition tests integrity.

True stewards do not abandon their post in adversity. They press on, anchored by hope and empowered by grace.

ENCOURAGEMENT FOR THE WEARY

Many grow weary in well-doing, but Galatians 6:9 promises: **"And let us not grow weary while doing good, for in due season we shall reap if we do not lose heart." (NKJV).**

God sees every hidden act of faithfulness. The steward who perseveres in prayer, service, generosity, and obedience will reap eternal reward.

MODERN APPLICATION

- A missionary serving for decades with little visible fruit but remaining faithful until the end.

- An elderly saint still praying daily, mentoring younger believers, and testifying of God's goodness.

- A Christian enduring persecution yet refusing to deny Christ.

- Parents remaining steadfast in raising children in faith despite cultural opposition.

Faithful stewardship is not glamorous—it is steady, enduring, and unshakable.

THE PROMISE FOR THE FAITHFUL

Revelation 2:10 declares: **"Be faithful until death, and I will give you the crown of life." (NKJV).**

God does not require perfection, but He does require perseverance. Those who remain faithful to the end will receive eternal honor.

REFLECTION

1. Are you committed to finishing the race of faith, or are you growing weary?

2. What trials tempt you to compromise your stewardship?

3. How can you strengthen endurance so that you remain faithful until the end?

4. If your life ended today, would you be found as one who kept the faith?

PRAYER

Lord, I desire not only to begin well but to finish strong. Strengthen me to remain faithful through trials, temptations, and seasons of weariness. Keep me from compromise and distraction. Like Paul, may I be able to say, **"I have fought a good fight, I have finished my course, I have kept the faith."** Crown me not for my strength, but for Your sustaining grace that carries me to the end. In Jesus' name. Amen.

Chapter 22

The Legacy of Stewardship

STEWARDSHIP BEYOND A LIFETIME

Stewardship does not end when we die. Our influence, choices, and faithfulness ripple into future generations. Proverbs 13:22 says: **"A good man leaves an inheritance to his children's children, but the wealth of the sinner is stored up for the righteous." (NKJV).** This inheritance is not only material—it is spiritual, moral, and eternal.

Every steward leaves a legacy: one of faithfulness that inspires others, or of negligence that warns others. The way we handle our time, talents, and treasures today shapes lives we may never meet on earth.

BIBLICAL EXAMPLES OF LEGACY

- Abraham left a legacy of faith that blessed generations (**see Genesis 22:18**).

- David left a legacy of worship and a royal lineage leading to Christ (**see Acts 13:22–23**).

- Timothy's grandmother, Lois, and mother, Eunice, passed down sincere faith to him (**see 2 Timothy 1:5**).

- The widow's offering still speaks centuries later, showing the power of sacrificial stewardship (**see Mark 12:43–44**).

Legacies are not measured by size but by faithfulness.

WHAT KIND OF LEGACY WILL WE LEAVE?

1. **A Legacy of Faith** – Do we leave behind a testimony that points others to Christ?

2. **A Legacy of Service** – Did our lives model humility, compassion, and sacrifice?

3. **A Legacy of Generosity** – Did we invest in eternal causes that continue after us?

4. **A Legacy of Truth** – Did we pass on sound doctrine, integrity, and holiness?

Every choice either strengthens or weakens the legacy we leave.

THE CONTRAST OF LEGACIES

- The rich fool built bigger barns but left no eternal impact (**see Luke 12:20–21**).

- Judas wasted his stewardship and left a legacy of betrayal.

- Paul poured out his life for the gospel and left letters that still guide the church today.

What we do with our stewardship will outlive us.

MODERN APPLICATION

- Parents modeling prayer and scripture reading for their children create a legacy of devotion.

- Believers who support missions leave a legacy that carries the gospel to nations.

- Servants in local churches who disciple others multiply their faith beyond their lifetime.

- Ordinary Christians living faithfully in daily life inspire others long after they are gone.

The greatest legacy is not in buildings, wealth, or recognition but in lives transformed for Christ.

LEAVING AN ETERNAL LEGACY

Psalm 112:6 says: **"The righteous will be in everlasting remembrance." (NKJV).** A faithful steward is remembered not for what they owned, but for what they gave, how they served, and whom they led to Christ.

At the end of life, the question will not be: *"How much did you accumulate?"* but rather: *"How much did you invest into eternity?"*

REFLECTION

1. What legacy are you currently building through your stewardship?

2. How will your children, church, or community remember you?

3. Are you leaving behind temporary possessions or eternal impact?

4. What steps can you take today to create a lasting, Christ-centered legacy?

PRAYER

Lord, I thank You for entrusting me with life, gifts, and opportunities. Please help me to live not only for today but for generations to come. Forgive me for moments of wasted stewardship. Teach me to invest my time, talents, and treasure in ways that will outlive me. May my legacy be one of faith, service, generosity, and truth. Let my life point others to You long after I am gone. In Jesus' name. Amen.

Conclusion

To Whom Much Is Given, Much Is Required

Throughout this journey, we have traced the weighty and glorious truth of Luke 12:48: **"For everyone to whom much is given, from him much will be required..."** **(NKJV).** We have seen that stewardship is not optional—it is the very essence of Christian living.

God has entrusted us with time, talent, treasure, relationships, opportunities, and above all, the gospel of Jesus Christ. These are not random blessings—they are divine assignments. Each resource carries a responsibility. Each blessing carries a burden of accountability.

THE CALL OF STEWARDSHIP

- In our personal lives, stewardship means living holy, disciplined, and intentional.

- In ministry and leadership, it means shepherding faithfully, without compromise, and with servant hearts.

- In the world, it means managing finances God's way, redeeming time, developing talents, giving generously, and serving with compassion.

- In eternity, it means knowing that every act will be weighed before the judgment seat of Christ.

Stewardship is not about perfection, but about faithfulness. God does not expect equal results from every believer, but He does expect obedience from every steward.

THE ETERNAL WEIGHT OF RESPONSIBILITY

We are reminded that this life is short, but eternity is forever. One day soon, Christ will return. On that day, excuses will vanish, opportunities will be closed, and only what was done for Him will matter.

The words **"Well done, good and faithful servant" (see Matthew 25:23)** are not given lightly. They are reserved for those who lived with eternity in view, who labored with faithfulness, who invested wisely, who served sacrificially, and who finished well.

May it not be said of us that we wasted our stewardship, buried our talents, or neglected the least of these. Instead, may we be found as faithful stewards who multiplied what God placed in our hands.

YOUR LEGACY OF STEWARDSHIP

Friend, your life is writing a legacy right now. Every decision, every act of service, every word spoken, every dollar spent, every soul you reach—it all counts. Your legacy is not only about what you leave behind but about what you send ahead into eternity.

The question is not if you are leaving a legacy, but what kind of legacy you are leaving. Will it be one of faith, obedience, and impact—or one of neglect and regret?

THE FINAL CHARGE

As we close this book, I leave you with a charge: Live as one entrusted.

- Steward your time wisely.
- Steward your talents faithfully.
- Steward your treasures generously.
- Steward your relationships lovingly.
- Steward the gospel urgently.

Do not waste the gift of life. Do not delay obedience. Do not bury what God has entrusted to you. Instead, live ready for the Master's return.

CLOSING PRAYER

Heavenly Father, I thank You for the life, gifts, and opportunities You have entrusted to me. I recognize that I am a steward, not an owner. Please help me to live with faithfulness, wisdom, and urgency. Teach me to redeem my time, to multiply my talents, to invest my treasure, and to serve others with compassion. Keep my heart pure, my hands diligent, and my eyes fixed on eternity. On that great day when I stand before You, may I hear the words, **"Well done, good and faithful servant."** In Jesus' name. Amen.

Scripture Reference Index

STEWARDSHIP AND ACCOUNTABILITY

- Luke 12:48
- Romans 14:10–12
- 1 Corinthians 4:2
- 2 Corinthians 5:10
- Hebrews 13:17

TIME AND OPPORTUNITY

- Ephesians 5:15–16
- John 9:4
- Matthew 25:1–13
- Galatians 6:9
- James 4:14

TALENT AND GIFTS

- 1 Peter 4:10
- Matthew 25:14–30
- Romans 12:6–8
- 1 Corinthians 12:4–7
- Colossians 3:23–24

FINANCES AND TREASURE

- Psalm 24:1
- Malachi 3:10
- Matthew 6:19–21
- Luke 16:11
- 1 Timothy 6:10
- Proverbs 11:25

SERVICE, COMPASSION, AND SACRIFICE

- Matthew 20:26–28
- Mark 10:45
- Matthew 25:35–40
- Philippians 2:4–8
- Acts 20:35
- James 1:27

LEADERSHIP AND RESPONSIBILITY

- Ezekiel 34:2–4
- John 21:15–17
- Acts 20:28–29
- 1 Peter 5:2–4
- Proverbs 29:25

PERSEVERANCE AND FAITHFULNESS

- 2 Timothy 4:7–8

- Matthew 24:13
- Hebrews 12:1–2
- Revelation 2:10
- Galatians 6:9

ETERNAL REWARDS AND CROWNS

- 1 Corinthians 3:12–15
- Revelation 22:12
- 2 Timothy 4:8
- 1 Thessalonians 2:19
- 1 Corinthians 9:25
- James 1:12
- 1 Peter 5:4
- Revelation 4:10

ETERNAL ACCOUNTABILITY

- Matthew 25:14–30
- Matthew 25:31–46
- 2 Corinthians 5:10
- 1 Corinthians 4:5
- 2 John 8